Life's Little Quirks

by

Helen M. Clarke

Contents

Life In The Slow Lane

Dogs, Humans And Other Creatures

Might As Well Laugh About It

Life In The Slow Lane

1. Forward Planning

I planned to do it yesterday
And then today instead
But now tomorrow makes more sense
- I like to think ahead

2. The Achievement

Right - take a deep breath, flex the muscles
Now concentrate, focus, prepare
Dive in – bold is best. Don't be timid
Take heart. Take control. Don't despair
… Okay, so that hurt. Yes, it's painful
But worth it – well, will be, in time
Deep breath. Try again. Flex those muscles
Remember. To fail is no crime
Yes, soreness is very unpleasant
And aching and throbbing no fun
But think of the feeling of triumph
And joy when the battle is won
… Admitting defeat's not an option
This challenge needs meeting *today*
There *must* be an answer – just find it
… Hot water! Of course. *That's* the way!
Okay. Try again. Flex those muscles
Now twist. Yes! It's turning at last!
The Bovril jar's finally open
Its lid is no longer stuck fast

3. My Memoirs

I thought I'd write my memoirs
- An easy thing to do –
My journals go back years and years
They're full of details too

Each visit to the dentist
Optician, doctor, vet
Those little errands, day by day
So easy to forget

The luxuries I've purchased
The birthday cakes I've baked
The bills I've paid, the housework done
The autumn leaves I've raked

The work-related problems
- And triumphs, all too rare –
The people I've had dealings with
(I mention these with care)

No gossip or disclosures
I live in constant dread
That prying eyes might read my notes
And frown on what I've said

I thought I'd write my memoirs
But then I changed my mind
To bore my readers half to death
Would not be very kind

4. Housework

The place is untidy, a bit of a mess
Junk, washing and pots lie in wait
The cobwebs are dusty – well housework's a bore
But who cares? It's home and it's *great*!

5. Recycling

Recycling - what a fuss they make!
It's really nothing new
I've hoarded junk for years in case
I need it - haven't *you*?

The garage, loft and garden shed
Are bursting at the seams
With clutter which might someday be
The answer to my dreams

I'm rather short of storage space
And so, I must confess -
With piles of useful stuff around
The house *is* quite a mess

But who knows when I'll need that box?
That lid? That piece of string?
And all those lovely plastic pots -
What pleasure *they* might bring!

I've made some splendid toys and games
From packaging and waste -
Cars - houses - crazy golf - from bits
That others dump in haste

Church notices make shopping lists
Glass jars store nails and screws
Old underwear makes cleaning cloths
… My plant pots once were shoes

Oh yes, I never throw things out
I'll always find a use
And now recycling's all the rage
I've got a great excuse!

6. Life in the Slow Lane

I'm really so busy
It's getting me down
I ran out of teabags
And walked into town
The house needed cleaning
But weariness won
I'll vacuum tomorrow
Then rest when it's done
There's lunch to prepare …
Plus an email to send
… Some plants to be watered …
The chores never end

I ought to start moving
There's so much to do
- I'll just take a moment
To think it all through

7. My New Gadget

I've got an amazing new gadget
It can't crash. It can't go offline
No need for computer or wi-fi
- A truly inventive design

No mind-boggling options or updates
No software, no passwords to hack
No reason for virus protection
No freezing, no cookies to track

No cables, no plugs, no recharging
No keys, mouse or buttons to press
And yet it can store lots of data
Without technological stress

This data is easily accessed
No file names to choose then forget
No service provider to thwart me
No spam, cons, scams, phishing or threat

No hardware to fail or malfunction
No cyber troll, no Trojan horse
This wonderful gadget? You've guessed it –
A notebook and pencil, of course

8. January 6ᵗʰ

Well Christmas time is over now
It came and then it went
I'm feeling rather bloated and
My money's all but spent

My trimmings, cards and larger gifts
Are heaped up on the floor
I put them in a cupboard but
I couldn't shut the door

I haven't sent my *Thank You*s yet
All day my conscience nags
I'm glad I made a note of
Who gave what, and kept the tags

The jobs I've left undone for weeks
Are yelling, "Do me NOW!"
There's no escape. Today's the day …
Tomorrow anyhow

Yes Christmas time is over and
I shed a little tear
… How comforting to know that
Christmas time will soon be here!

9. The Clear-Out

It's time for a clear-out
I've got too much stuff
My cupboards and drawers are replete
The floor space is shrinking
The corners have gone
To find them will be quite a feat

I'll start with my wardrobe
… I never wear *that*
Though - maybe – it still looks quite smart
I'll keep it for now
But that jumper can go …
Perhaps … No, I haven't the heart

My bookcase is groaning
With books never read
How many, in truth, do I need?
That thick tome on fungi?
The one about gems?
That volume on sheep, every breed?

But thinking about it –
Those items, all three
Were gifts from a friend I hold dear
To ditch them is callous
Unfeeling and cold
Their rightful place, frankly, is here

So on to my "treasures"
No. They'll have to stay
Their sentiment value is high
My music's essential
My DVDs too
I'll come to my shoes by and by

Ah! Paper! Rough scrawlings
Lists, memos, receipts
Recycling bin, that's where *you'll* go!
A tatty old folder
I no longer use
- My hard work is starting to show

A biro, now empty
A rubber gone hard
Two paper clips tangled and bent
A broken container
A bag full of holes
My toothbrush! So *that's* where it went!

Wow! That was a challenge
But well worth the time
All day – well it wasn't a race
It's strangely refreshing
To sort through your stuff
Just one snag – I've still got no space!

10. The Art of Giving Directions

"Please – could you direct me to Westminster Drive?
My Sat Nav denies its existence"
"Um – yes – let me think. You're the wrong side of town
You'll still have to go quite a distance
Keep heading straight north till you come to a bend
Ignore that – it's not where you're going
Then turn left soon after, but not by the pub
You should see some red bunting blowing

Then carry on down through the shops and beyond
Make sure you pass Waitrose and Aldi
You'll come to a crossroads, at which you turn right
And round by that wall that looks mouldy
Now – Westminster Drive – well, it's *somewhere* round there
It's noisy, and busy with traffic
I think there's a show place – computers and stuff
Look out for a fast-moving graphic
And if you find *that* you're a few streets away
So follow your nose round The Crescent
And sooner or later you'll come to a park
It's small, but surprisingly pleasant
You don't want the park, so keep driving along
Two minutes if moving quite quickly
Should bring you to *something* – a café? – That's right
The cakes are good value but sickly
Well, once you get *there*, my advice is to ask
You don't want to waste time exploring
So glad I could help. If you searched on your own
It really would get rather boring"

Dogs, Humans And Other Creatures

11. An Honest Canine Mistake
by Sam

On a coffee table
Sitting on a plate
Was a lonely little cake
In quite a sorry state

No one seemed to want it
The other cakes had gone
I didn't see the need to ask
I scoffed it down in one

My humans started yelling
They sent me from the room
I got the feeling they were cross
It filled my heart with gloom

I couldn't understand it
The cake was *meant* for me
Perhaps I was supposed to wait
And have it for my tea

12. The Joys of a New Puppy

You jump out of bed every morning
No lie-ins – there's too much at stake
A howling below makes you hurry
It's Puppy, half-starved and awake

You sit down to look at the paper
A ball crashes into your feet
The flinger stands waiting for action
It's Puppy - meek, gentle and sweet

You're having a snooze, all is peaceful
You suddenly wake with a jerk
As loud, high-pitched barks break the silence
It's Puppy, the watchdog, at work

You're sipping a hot cup of coffee
Sharp teeth clamp your fingers with force
It's time for some rough stuff, quite clearly
Your playmate? Yes, Puppy, of course

You're crocheting, watching the telly
The wool doesn't come when you tug
You find it's been pounced on and hijacked
By Puppy, your own little thug

It's chilly and murky and bitter
Your warm, cosy home's out of reach
For you're up the road getting frozen
With Puppy, your delicate peach

It's quarter past ten in the evening
A baby's asleep in your arm
A cuddly, adorable bundle
It's Puppy, contented and calm

13. Tips for My Human from a Misunderstood Pooch
by Charlie

I'd like to begin on a high note
And praise you – for praise *is* your due
For being a slave to be proud of
Devoted, indulgent and true

Psychology, though, is a problem
Your knowledge of mine is unsound
Chihuahua-with-papillon psyche
Is complex, exquisite, profound

I can't expect *full* understanding
To do so would be most unfair
But sometimes your lack of compassion
Reduces my heart to despair

To give an example which pains me
I grrr in affection or fun
And you reel in horror, and scold me
For some alleged wrong that I've done

And if I advance with my gnashers
You wince and retreat like a frog
- You're *meant* to lunge back in excitement
And play-fight, with teeth, dog to dog

My needs are quite simple and modest
I really don't ask much of you
- Respect, patience, tolerance, calmness
Complaisance and deference too

Your sympathy-empathy reading
Is, sad to say, well below par
Regarding my delicate feelings
It grieves me how clueless you are

So if you aspire to perfection
- The best a mere human can be –
You do need to try a bit harder
To fully appreciate me

14. The Wall

I know he didn't mean it
I know he's racked with guilt
He bumped the wall and down it went
It needs to be rebuilt

He said he'd get it sorted
- I'm sure he meant it too –
He made some phone calls, took some snaps
And sent his photos through

"I've set the wheels in motion
- Next Monday at a guess"
A few weeks passed. Then someone came
To tidy up the mess

"I'll clear away the rubble
But building's not my thing
I'll make arrangements. Don't despair
I'll give my pal a ring …

He'll come a week on Tuesday
- Or Thursday. Thereabouts
Look, here's my number. Get in touch
If ever you have doubts"

A few weeks passed. No action
The neighbours thought the worst
A phone call proved them wrong
"Oh yes, we have a list. *You're* first

A week or so should do it"
A week or so went by
… A few more weeks … a month … two months
It did no good to cry

I know he means to fix it
I know he's racked with guilt
And maybe in a year or two
The wall *will* be rebuilt

15. The Techno-Wizard

A genius needs no instructions
A bright techno-wizard like you
Embraces new challenges gladly
And always knows just what to do

Install a new gadget – no problem
Three bits to plug in? Never fear
Just force them – it won't really matter
Ignore any sizzling you hear

Click here to delete all your settings
That's fine – we can soon get them back
No knowledge or training are needed
A genius just has the knack

Remote controls not really working?
Need programming? Easy for some
One minor adjustment – press *Volume*
- The clock on the wall starts to hum

Press *Mute* and you lose all the colour
Press *Sky* and the lights all come on
Press *Green* and the printer starts printing
Press *Red* and the internet's gone

Your e-reader pages keep freezing
That's fixed with one magical touch
All text can be speedily accessed
No longer in English, but Dutch

The phone won't make contact with others
Since needing a Techno-Wiz tweak
But now when you key in a number
The grill heats – that's surely unique

Now switches – they *can* pose a problem
Despite all your technical flair
Which switch do you flick for some music?
To turn on the lamp near the chair?

But don't let small mishaps distress you
You know there's no end to your skill
And if you keep fiddling and coaxing
Most gizmos will bend to your will

16. The Careful Dresser

Now some think they're safe in *all* weathers
As long as they cover their arms
They just grab a coat from the cupboard
And set off without any qualms

But *you* know it's not that straightforward
There's so much to think of and plan
- Prepare for a gale, fiercely arctic
A roasting, or even a tan

You're wise to the need to determine
The speed and direction of wind
Correct choice of hat is essential
- And should it be tied on or pinned?

A gentle breeze calls for a beanie
Bright sun for a cap with a peak
Northeaster - then penguin hat triumphs
With muffler for mouth, nose and cheek

And just in case reason proves faulty
And errors of judgement occur
You know an alternative's vital
- Full mask, balaclava, fake fur

Secreted in pocket, quite neatly
These extras are crucial, it's clear
The wrong hat can cause angst and hardship
The right one brings comfort and cheer

But which coat? Now *that's* a dilemma
So much to take into account -
Wind, temperature, wetness or dryness
If wetness, what sort? What amount?

Long raincoat for total protection
Thick overcoat, really for best
Light jacket, so thin and quite draughty
But fine with a waterproof vest

Old anorak, eager and faithful
Strong, sturdy, although rather short
With hood poised to spring into action
If in dicey weather you're caught

Now legs are a serious problem
Just how many layers should you wear?
Socks, knee warmers, trousers and leggings?
These things must be worked out with care

But long johns, without any question
Research it - you'll certainly find -
With prophet-like anticipation
Were dreamed up with *your* needs in mind

Of course, there are other decisions
Like footwear and thickness of scarf
But if these are paid due attention
Stress levels are lowered by half

So dressing for outdoor adventure
Is thrilling and never a chore
In summer allow twenty minutes
In winter an hour or more

17. The Meditator

You might think he's sleeping and out for the count
You might think that noise is his snoring
You might think the stupor in which he resides
Is slumber resistant to pawing
You might think he's dreaming and not in control
Of grunting and twitching and speaking
You might think he's slumped for an afternoon snooze
You might think his sensors need tweaking
You might think you ought to be silent and still
For fear that you'll cause him to waken
You might think he's lost in the great land of Nod
And truth is you won't be mistaken

18. Christmas Greetings

A "Happy Christmas" greeting
From Bill and Barbie Bray
We're sure you're keen to read our news
So here goes – no delay
It's been a year of troubles
The longed-for cruise fell through
We both went down with viruses
Then Bill had full-blown flu
The children keep us busy
(Though adults now, of course)
Rebecca broke an arm and leg
When falling off her horse

Poor Bob's been made redundant
Patricia crashed her car
She'll soon be out of hospital
But all her cuts will scar
Our house was broken into
And struck by lightning too
The damage was extensive and
There's still a lot to do
Old Uncle Ned is failing
He won't be with us long
Bill's sister's had a breakdown
(Well, her nerves were never strong)
Our nephew's been arrested
He's innocent, of course
It's just a little mix-up
In the midst of his divorce
Well, that's our festive update
Enjoy the Christmas cheer
Have fun this special happy time
And through the coming year

19. In the Still of the Night

In the still and the chill of a bright moonlit night
He awoke and reluctantly stirred
To the bathroom he staggered, then back to his bed
- Where he found something strange had occurred
In his place was a body – a large one at that
With its head on the pillow, eyes shut
And the duvet wrapped round it. So cosy. So snug
The usurper? His warmth-loving mutt

20. For the Sake of the Spiders

It's tricky to clean in the corners
And cruel to brush cobwebs away
Can't bear to upset all those spiders
So mucky is how it will stay!

21. Hedgehog's Encounter

A hedgehog woke, the sun was low
"It's getting dark," he thought
"I'd better go and find some food"
He gave a little snort

He headed for the patio
Where hedgehog found each night
A tasty feast and water too
He ran with all his might

He hurried down the garden path
And cut across the lawn
"There's such a lot to do," he sighed
"Before the crack of dawn"

But what was that? A fluffy mound!
The hedgehog gulped, "How mean!
A cat! It's scoffing all my grub!"
He hurtled to the scene

"Hey, have a heart," the hedgehog cried
"That meal was meant for me"
"Just wait your turn," the cat replied
"I didn't get much tea"

The hedgehog circled round and round
Then gave the cat a biff
"Just hold your horses!" puss exclaimed
"I'll only be a jiff"

Poor hedgehog went to have a drink
He lapped at quite a pace
Then tipped the dish towards him – *splat*!
It smacked him in the face

He felt so wet he shook and shook
The cat got splashed and fled
The dish of food was still quite full
"Now *my* turn!" hedgehog said

22. Frog's Expedition

"I'll go on a big expedition"
Thought frog. "To the hedge and beyond"
The day was just right for an outing
But first to get out of the pond

He swam to the top of the water
And paused for a moment to think
Then sploshed to the bottom in terror
A bird had come down for a drink

The bird flew away, frog felt safer
He wriggled his way to the top
A human strolled into the garden –
And down went the frog with a plop

"Hey, this isn't funny," frog grumbled
"Don't humans and birds ever *sleep*?"
He eased himself out of the water
Preparing to take a big leap

"That's better," he told himself firmly
"No need for this worry and doubt"
- He gulped and dived into the water
A squirrel was bouncing about

"Forget it!" gasped frog in frustration
"I'll stay where I am. *I* don't care!"
The pond was calm, cosy and quiet
And frog really *loved* it in there

23. Grumblings of a Grey Squirrel

I seem to be unpopular
Which surely isn't fair
I air the lawn by digging holes
And store my food with care
I really can't imagine why
Folk want to shoo me off
I'm not the only garden guest
Who likes to sit and scoff

Those birds are always tucking in
They're greedy *and* they're rude
I know they'd rather watch me starve
Than let me share their food
Yet no one gets annoyed with *them*
Or sends them on their way
I sometimes think this persecution's
All because I'm grey
It's just as well I'm strong and brave
And birds are weak and shy
By barging in I get some nuts –
One step and off they fly
Their table's quite a challenge, though
I get inside the bowl
By jumping from the apple tree
Or shinning up the pole
I'm such a splendid acrobat
I'm handsome and I'm smart
I'm lots of fun as well, so
Come on, humans – have a heart

24. Four-and-Twenty Blackbirds
(*give or take a few*)

My garden is a paradise
Or so it would appear
A place where blackbirds feel at home
In hunger, joy and fear

One day I counted nine – I think
Then two more joined the throng
Four ladies, seven blokes at least
Too busy, all, for song

The females often number six
- A couple hid that day -
… So *thirteen* blackbirds, could be more
Determined, all, to stay

They dash about, such anguished birds
Through bushes, round the lawn
They come and go - like magic, some
… All day, to dusk from dawn

They chase and squabble, squawk and fight
Yet no one seems to reign
At times they're almost tolerant
Though sharing is a strain

How lost I'd feel, how desolate
How sorry I would be
If ever I looked out and
Not one blackbird could I see

25. The Clever Crow

A hungry crow was searching round
For something nice to eat
Ah, what was that? A large bread roll!
Bread rolls were quite a treat

The crow swooped down to claim its prize
But what a nasty shock!
The roll was dry and very hard
And solid as a rock

"Good job my beak's so strong," thought crow
"I have no magic wand"
Crow stabbed the roll, then picked it up
And dropped it in the pond

Crow waited calmly while it soaked
Then fished it out with glee
Crow feasted well and flew away
As happy as could be

26. Rooftop Tussle

The strangest thing happened one morning
I glanced through the window and spied
A crow on a neighbouring rooftop
An object, quite large, at its side

I grabbed my binoculars swiftly
Not certain I wanted to know
What loot would be valued so highly
By corpse-eating carrion crow

Bread roll! Phew! Relief filled my being
Then crow seemed to cower. With *fright*?
Though clearly discomfited greatly
Crow made no attempt to take flight

But what would alarm and unsettle
A crow – who could sparrowhawks chase?
- A magpie touched down on the rooftop
Invading the feasting crow's space

So that was it! Covetous magpie
Crow's booty was eager to pinch
Bold magpie danced round, seeking access
Crow, wary but calm, didn't flinch

Pert magpie, determined yet nervous
Skipped closer, but didn't dare snatch
And, circling, discovered that magpies
For wise, composed crows are no match

Now crow near the roof's edge was standing
So when magpie hopped to the brink
Crow biffed, with a human like elbow
And malice aforethought, in sync

Poor magpie, decisively ousted
Plunged down to a small, spindly tree
Convinced by crow's eloquent message
Awed magpie decided to flee

27. Osbert

The cat had gone missing
They searched high and low
In buckets and plant pots
Behind rake and hoe

They emptied their cupboards
And waste bins and drawers
And combed rugs and carpets
For whiskers and claws

They peered up the chimney
They poked down the drain
They pulled out the bookcase
And wardrobe in vain

They begged friends and neighbours
To check in their sheds
And inside their ovens
And under their beds

But Osbert had vanished
No clue could be found
They called and beseeched him
But puss made no sound

They turned to the kettle
In need of a drink
And there was old Osbert
Asleep in the sink

28. Puss on Hutch

Poor puss, I've learned you have no home
You're hungry, sad, just left to roam
You're chasing birds and hunting mice
Which really *isn't* very nice
And so I'll feed you if you cease
And leave my birds and mice in peace
You hang around outside the door
- I have a hunch I know what for
You'd like to come inside, I guess
But that would cause my dog distress

He wouldn't want to share with you
Just take my word. It's harsh but true
And yet I do feel rather mean
In spite of what a pest you've been
You need a place to call your own
You're lost, forlorn and all alone
And so I've bought a special hutch
For outdoor cats – for strays and such
It heats itself and has a flap
Your own warm room to take a nap
I've put it near the house for you
- It's kind of like you live here too –
Come on. Let's see you go inside
A safe, dry den in which to hide
I've made it snug. Just look and see
Now try it … Go on … *Please* … For *me*
… You silly cat. You're foolish. *Rude*
I've left it open, stocked with food
You sit on top – and that's no sin -
But *still* refuse to venture in
Puss, use your brains, your common sense
It seems to me you're rather dense
This hutch is *yours*, a cosy bed
Don't choose the cold and damp instead
… Well, when you're frozen, awkward cat
It's not *my* fault. Remember *that*!

29. Feline Friend

Those dainty paws and striking eyes
That soft and soothing fur
Those special tender moments and
That traction engine purr

Proud puss, so self-contained and sure
Contrary to the core
And always - by coincidence?
The wrong side of the door!

Knows just what's what and what should be
Wise, complex, private, deep
Aloof and independent, yet
So snuggly when asleep

A cat - such poise and dignity
Intelligence and grace
A loving and devoted friend
Who keeps you in your place

30. Canine Companion

That cold wet nose, those eager eyes
That soothing, nuzzling touch
A special pal, who worships you
And never asks for much -

Just lots of love - attention - food
Fun - games - and treats galore
Long walks - good smells - a comfy bed
And something nice to gnaw ...

So optimistic, full of joy
With pooch life's never dull
Enthusiasm fills the air
With hardly any lull

Oh yes, a dog's great company
And entertaining too
A faithful and devoted friend
Whose world revolves round you

31. A Dog's Musings

I've come to the weighty conclusion
That humans are somewhat bizarre
Their habits are rather disturbing
And show how erratic they are

Mine settle each evening for crosswords
And *cross* are the words they exchange
They groan and they grumble and grizzle
For something that's *fun*? Now *that's* strange

They go for a walk – which is normal -
But stop to converse with their friends
If *I* talk to *dogs* I'm in trouble
Such conduct, quite frankly, offends

I see humans passing the window
With gadgets plugged into their ears
While fiddling with something they're holding
Or speaking to no one who hears

My own humans have many gadgets
And none of them work as they should
One press of a button … disaster!
I'd throw them away if I could

They put plants indoors – *trees* at Christmas!
Where scents worth exploring don't land
Their primary use is forbidden
And that I just can't understand

So dealing with humans is tricky
Brave tolerance goes a long way
Strong, patient resolve is essential
Resilient hearts win the day

32. Dog Walking

Now *I'm* the human. *I'm* in charge
You'll walk the path *I* choose
We'll go home when *I* say we will
Don't challenge or refuse
Good dog. Turn left – No! *Left* I said
This yank means *Come With Me*
Don't pull against me. *Left* I said
Don't drag me to that tree
Okay. Turn right if that's your wish
But next time *I* decide
I mean it. No more nonsense now
Don't undermine my pride
No. *Don't* cross over. Walk straight on
This road's too busy. *Stay*!
… Okay, if you insist, we'll cross
- It might well take all day
I hate this road … You'll have to *wait*
It's *your* fault. Don't blame *me*
We could be way up there by now
If you had *sense* you'd see

At last we're over, safe and sound
Where now? What's in your mind?
Don't dither or I'll take you home
… No. That would be unkind
Okay. Where next? It's up to you
I'll let you lead the way
But *I'm* in charge. Remember that
I have the final say

Might As Well Laugh About It

33. Sparkling Clean

The window couldn't see outside
I squirted it with spray
Then rubbed it dry, the way I should
The splodges chose to stay

I sprayed again, and rubbed and scrubbed
My arm began to ache
I sprayed and rubbed and sprayed and scrubbed
No difference did it make

I drank a soothing cup of tea
Then set to work once more
My neck and shoulder throbbed with pain
My fingertips were sore

At last – a breakthrough! One by one
The splodges lost their fight
My window sparkled, gleamed and shone
The world looked clear and bright

But as I gazed in pure delight
The sun sent out a beam
My sparkling window shone no more
No longer did it gleam

The splodges had, indeed, dispersed
But gloating in their place
Were streaks and smears and blurry lines
Which mocked my anguished face

I squirted them and rubbed them hard
To show them who was boss
The smears and streaks just grew and spread
- I pulled the blind across

34. Shopper's Riddle

The bags were surprisingly heavy
I'd spent all my money – well nearly
But checking my list I discovered
I hadn't bought *anything* really!

35. Trials and Tribulations of a Leicester City Fan
In loving memory of club chairman Vichai Srivaddhanaprabha

The Foxes are winning
No – hang on – that's wrong
They're playing quite well
But resistance is strong

They keep missing chances
The net taunts and leers
The fans long for action
The players for cheers

No! Scandal! Disaster!
The Arsenal has scored
Result of a foul
Which the ref just *ignored*

Now *that* was a penalty
Surely. A gem
The ref favours Arsenal
He's playing for *them*!

Catastrophe! Heartache!
The Gunners have won
The Foxes was robbed
Fifteenth game on the run

36. Faithful Daily Newspaper

Emotive, unreliable
Inaccurate and woolly
Misleading, biased, badly wrote
Sport not reported fully
While other teams are fussed about
And eulogised and fêted
Poor Leicester City's feats are
Overlooked and underrated
The crossword clues are dubious
And really not that clever
News coverage is patchy – not
A whiff of our town ever
Insulting to the intellect
Fake wisdom nought but vapour
How empty life would be without
Our faithful daily paper!

37. Knitting Prowess

I thought I'd knit a blanket
… A scarf … Perhaps a hat
I didn't have much wool
But I could make a little mat

The stitches kept increasing
Which didn't bother *me*
Whatever was I making?
I'd just have to wait and see

My Thing was getting longer
And wider by the row
Its shape was still unclear
But what a thrill to watch it grow

My ball of wool was shrinking
To cast off would be wise
… A cosy for an egg cup …
What a wonderful surprise!

I folded it and stitched it
My heart was filled with pride
I'd left a little opening
To push the egg inside

- Yet to this day my knitwear
Has never clothed an egg
For what I'd made, unknowing
Was a cosy for a peg

I hadn't sensed a problem
That someone ought to fix
… But maybe I should mention
I was only five or six

38. Catastrophic Culinary Crisis

"A Ruby Anniversary!
This calls for cake," she thought
"I'll take some to the Thursday group
Home-made, of course. Not bought"

She doubled the ingredients
This cake would be the best
The largest, lightest, tastiest
Of sponges in the West

She cooked it till it turned light brown
Then made some butter cream
And stuck some cherries on the top
Sighed she, "It looks a dream!"

It seemed a little overweight
Laughed Hazel, "Don't we all?
It looks okay and smells just fine
Oh yes, we'll have a ball"

She took it to the Thursday group
It didn't want to cut
She gulped, "I hope it won't cause
Any damage to the gut"

The ladies tucked in heartily
But then began to choke
"This cake's delicious," someone gasped
Cried Hazel, "Please don't joke!"

They made kind comments, one and all
But didn't ask for more
"I'll take it home to finish off"
She said with aching jaw

She tried it on the folks at home
"It's *awful!*" spluttered one
"We don't deserve this punishment
Whatever's going on?"

She offered it to Sam, the dog
He viewed it with dismay
So, scared the cake would kill the birds
She threw the rest away

39. Be Warned

This nut bar is scrumptious, delicious
Its fibre will clear out your guts
You'll never taste anything like it
- Be warned, though, it might contain nuts

Let sleeping pills solve all your problems
No need to feel restless or lousy
These pills work their magic in seconds
- Be warned, though, they might make you drowsy

This poison will kill weeds and insects
It's merciless, lethal and quick
All pests will be vanquished - be warned, though
If swallowed it might make you sick

40. Of Sound Mind

I'm not superstitious. Such logic's absurd
Life can't be controlled by a thought, deed or word
I'd never succumb to irrational fears
Or let "signs" and "omens" reduce me to tears
I'm bright and well-balanced, my judgement is good
I'm solid and mentally healthy – touch wood
I walk under ladders to show I don't care
And choose number thirteen (then say a quick prayer)
I don't count my chickens – well, that would tempt fate
Or make rash assumptions - far better to wait
Black cats are a puzzle. Good luck or a curse?
Forgetting their meaning seems boldly perverse
Lone magpies – for sorrow? – don't fill me with dread
I just find a second, to bring *joy* instead
Well-disciplined thinking avoids any threat
That wild, careless wishes might lead to regret
Avoidance is sensible. Everyone knows
That playing it safe wards off jinxes and woes
Oh yes, I take pride, though perhaps I sound vain
In being of sound mind and totally sane

41. Dubious Friends

A carpet of yellow
A golden delight
So cheerful and friendly
Heart-warmingly bright
Resilient, faithful
Determined to fight
Despised dandelions
A glorious sight!

42. Spelling Maid Easy

I love my knew spell cheque
Its sew on the bawl
It nose wen I hit a wrong quay
It altars my errors
Without being tolled
Result: Perfect text, as ewe sea

43. Computer Updates

New updates are available
Click here to choose *Install*
It might take fifty minutes
- Or it might not work at all

Installing ... Please wait patiently
Just watch the bar progress
If *Error Message* intercepts
You'll know you're in a mess

Your internet connection's blipped
Click *Cancel*, then *Retry*
Installing ... Please wait patiently
And watch the moments fly

Installing ... Please wait patiently
Installing ... No, it's not ...
The bar's stopped moving. UPDATE FAILED
It's missed out quite a lot

Click *Cancel*. Then wait patiently
Click *Retry*. Oops! Bad luck
It's not responding. Click *Restart*
No good. The cursor's stuck

The screen's gone blank. No messages
Can't back up, print or save
Can't log off, shut down, access files
The situation's grave

New updates are available
But they're no use to me
I've nowhere to install them –
My computer's ceased to be!

44. My Trusty Computer

My trusty computer
My mentor, my friend
My helper, my playmate, my boss
You make your own judgements
And no doubt mean well
But flouting commands makes me cross
You think you know better
And go your own way
But sometimes you're on the wrong track
Note: ENTER means *keep*
Not *re-format* or *change*
- You do need to learn to hold back
I copy a rota
You alter the dates
Your logic for that is unclear
Replacing what's typed
Is high-handed and brash
You're great – but please don't interfere
I'm eagerly typing
But nothing appears
You're on a *Go Slow*, so I wait
It's very frustrating
My train of thought's gone
This stubbornness, frankly, I hate
And sometimes you pester
Yes, pester's the word
With prompts to update and install
I don't know their meaning
What choices to make
And you give no guidance at all

I love you and need you
So don't take offence
If sometimes I seem rather rude
It's just that your antics
And arrogant ways
Can put me in quite a bad mood!

45. No Internet Connection

If you can't get online, never fear, don't despair
Solutions aplenty are waiting
Just visit our website and click "Online Help"
Then give a review and star rating

If you can't get online, send an email to "Tech"
Explaining your problems connecting
We'll search for an answer and get back in touch
- Your router might need re-directing

If you can't get online, visit Facebook and such
To find out what others are doing
They'll tell you their woes, give you tips and advice
And warn you if trouble is brewing

If you can't get online, if your internet's down
And access to Google is lacking
Well, truth is, you're stuck. Please make sure you're online
And then you'll enjoy our full backing

46. Instructions

These came in thirteen languages
Though none of them my own
Good job I've got a great translation
Feature on my phone:

Instructions must be careful stalked
And carried off right through
If any wordings find ignored
Big danger will ensue

Make sure device is well in box
And all its bits are place
Put all together as is show
By picture under face

Connect to plug correct way up
If down no work will be
Press On. Red light will flash then not
Green light will tell to see

Choose option for your want to do
But wait for blue light wink
Beware not touch what saying should
Or if you taste bad stink

When all is ripe can use with fun
Ring help if nothing know
Watch heavy green for queueing off
And now you're up and go

47. Weathering the Weather

There's no point in moaning and groaning
We can't choose what weather we get
So *I* just accept what we're given
With humour and grace. *I* don't fret

You see, *I'm* no fair weather person
I greet life with courage each day
Inclement or fine, *I'm* not bothered
I'll weather it all, come what may

Except – well, we need rain, no question
But why can't it stick to the night?
Wet clothing is not just unpleasant
It has to be draped. What a sight!

Bright sunshine is cheering but irksome
It dazzles and waters the eyes
My nose burns and glows like a beacon
In seconds it sizzles and fries

Dark cloud cover makes me uneasy
A sinister threat's in the air
It gives me a sense of foreboding
And baffles me – what should I wear?

Now thunder and lightning are scary
The thought of them fills me with dread
But making a fuss would be silly
I simply retreat to my bed

Strong winds - even weak ones – are dicey
They're treacherous, evil, unkind
Their bullying ways are quite brutal
- A nice gentle breeze I don't mind

Fresh snowflakes descending look pretty
The ground, newly covered, delights
But slipping's no fun, nor is freezing
Snow's cold and it's wet and it BITES

Now fog is a bit of a hazard
And though I would never complain
I do like to see where I'm going
So fog's best avoided, like rain

To weather the weather is easy
- If *warm* (neither chilly nor hot)
Dry, calm, bright but shaded – no problem
I'll weather it, no matter what

48. Dilemma

That choc-chip cookie looks so sad
Just sitting on the plate
Its friends have long since disappeared
… So what of this one's fate?
I can't just leave it all alone
Forlorn inside a tin
Perhaps I ought to eat it *now*
- I *could*. I *am* quite thin

I've wolfed down two already
(As have others, not just *me*)
And, truth to tell, I'm rather full
So could I manage *three*?
- But this one looks so lonely, lost
Rejected, snubbed and spurned
Misgivings don't just fly away
(Life's wisdoms I have learned)
To leave it would be sensible
We all know that, of course
But if it feels unwanted – that
Would fill me with remorse
… There's nothing for it. Duty calls
My conscience is my guide
I'll eat it, for the greater good
And glow with righteous pride

49. The Wrapper Challenge

There's nothing to pick at, to pull or to tear
I can't get it open. It just isn't fair
No rough bits. No edges. I can't find a seam
I'm close to despair. Any moment I'll scream
There *must* be a join and a slit or a fold
A weak spot, some access, a loose bit to hold
I won't let it beat me. I can't let it win …
A sharp pair of scissors … I'll *snip* my way in
I've made an incision – well, gouged a small hole
I feel quite triumphant - in sight of my goal

A few tiny nicks. Not much progress as yet
A miniscule fragment is all I can get
But … yes! There's another! It's coming at last
Another … another … the crisis has passed
I've done it! It's open! The wrapping is off
I've conquered my foe – though I don't like to scoff
… Now what's *this*? A stiff band of plastic. Oh, *great*!
I've found what I needed, twelve minutes too late
- That sneaky, elusive, ingenious strip
That whips round like magic and works like a zip

50. Taking it Easy

I'm due for a lie-in
I've earned one for sure
Life's been pretty hectic of late
Today there's no hurry
No need to get up
No job to be done that can't wait

I'll lie back in comfort
Relax and drift off
There's no pressing business at stake
I'll relish each moment
Of blissful repose …
- It's no good. I'm too wide awake!

Other Titles By Helen M. Clarke

Life's Wonders And Riches
40 rhyming, rhythmic poems - a mixture of light-hearted and serious - celebrating and reflecting on life.

Charlie's A To Y
A dog's definitions in verse.

Canine Confusions And Feline Frustrations
A cat and dog saga told through the animals' emails.
Rescue dog Scruff has just moved into a new home, where resident cat Cleopatra reigns supreme. To Scruff's surprise, Cleopatra doesn't seem particularly thrilled to have him around. As Scruff and Cleopatra try to come to terms with their new living arrangements, Scruff exchanges emails with worldly-wise Maxie, his friend from the Pound, while Cleopatra corresponds with her devoted sister Tallulah.

Mince Pies And Paper Chains
A collection of 22 rhyming poems, 12 short stories and 6 miscellaneous prose pieces, all on a Christmas theme.

The Christmas Love Tree
A gentle story with a Christian slant. Newly retired Geraldine is thoroughly enjoying her freedom and the chance to be self-indulgent, although she is becoming increasingly aware of an unsettling feeling of emptiness and aimlessness. When she offers to help two children with their entry for the local Christmas Tree Festival she has no idea what a profound impact her involvement with their Christmas Love Tree will have on her life.

"With Love And Best Wishes..."
An affectionate skit on the round-robin Christmas letter.

Christmas Uncancelled
A gentle Christmas story, suitable for children and adults.
Christmas is going to be awful. Lynette's parents have gone on holiday and left her with old-fashioned Auntie Dorothy and pesky little Johnny. To make matters worse, the neighbours are acting strangely and Lynette is sure they're up to no good. Lynette prepares herself for a miserable time. She has no intention of even trying to enjoy herself. But will she really be able to stay grumpy throughout Christmas?

Another Move, Another Church
A series of rhyming, rhythmic poems depicting a year in the life of a small English church, seen through the eyes of the minister's teenage daughter.

Honest With God
Poems and reflections for worship and private devotions, focusing on Life's Ups and Downs and Through the Year.

Noah Gets It Right
15 poems retelling Bible stories in a light-hearted, colloquial style.

Verses For Greeting Cards
100 rhyming poems, with no copyright restrictions, for use in card making.

More Verses For Greeting Cards
A second collection of rhyming poems, with no copyright restrictions, for use in card making. A companion to the first collection.

Verses For Birthday And Christmas Cards
65 rhyming poems, with no copyright restrictions, for use in card making. There are 35 birthday verses (12 of which are for children) and 30 Christmas verses (6 for children).

11709380R00034

Printed in Great Britain
by Amazon